Strategic Planning Workbook

Strategic Planning Workbook

for Nonprofit Organizations

Bryan W. Barry

Amherst H. Wilder Foundation

This workbook was developed by
Management Support Services, a program
of the Amherst H. Wilder Foundation that
provides management consultation,
management training, accounting, and
other support services to nonprofit
organizations. The Amherst H. Wilder
Foundation is a large social service
organization with a staff of one thousand
providing direct and indirect health and
social services to people and organizations in the St. Paul community.
The foundation also serves as a resource
for nonprofit organizations throughout the
country.

We thank Dr. George Steiner, Dr. Robert
Allio, and others for their thoughtful
critique of this book. We also thank the
Publishing Center for Cultural Resources
for their assistance in producing the
Workbook, and First Bank Saint Paul and
First Bank Minneapolis for their funding of
development costs.

We hope you find this workbook helpful.
Should you need additional information
write or call Management Support
Services, Amherst H. Wilder Foundation,
919 Lafond Avenue, St. Paul, MN 55104,
phone 612/642-4025.

Designed by Christopher Holme

Drawings by Giora Carmi

Produced by Publishing Center for
Cultural Resources, New York City

Manufactured in the United States of
America

Table of Contents

1

Introduction to Strategic Planning

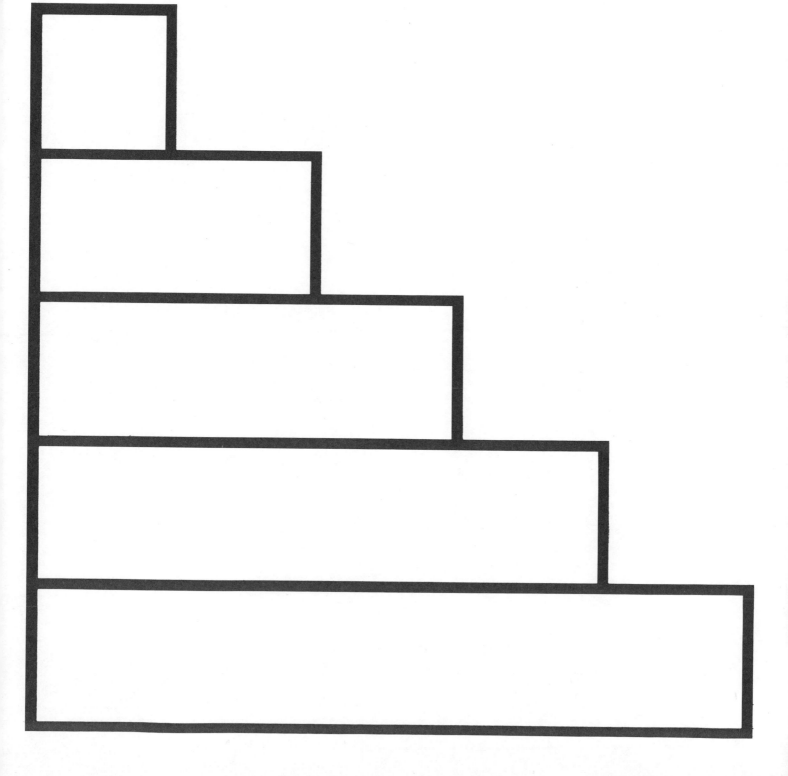

Since the early 1980s increasing numbers of nonprofit organizations have developed strategic plans. The most frequent consulting and training request we have received since then has been for help with strategic planning. Our colleagues around the country report similar interest.

Why are growing numbers of nonprofits doing strategic planning? Funding cuts, increased competition, and other pressures are forcing some organizations to plan for their very survival. Growing emphasis on sound management leads others to consider strategic planning, a practice widely used in for-profit corporations for over twenty years. Management assistance organizations, funders, and universities increasingly promote strategic planning as a management tool needed by today's nonprofit organizations.

We receive calls for planning help from about every kind of nonprofit organization—from grassroots groups to large city and county governments. A phone conversation might begin:

"Our financial situation is very tight this year and looks dismal next year. We've got to find a way out."

"My board chair (or a funder) is urging me to develop a long-range plan for our agency, but I'm not sure where to begin. To be honest, I'm a bit skeptical about the whole idea."

"We're facing stiffer competition for dollars and clients. We want to stay ahead of the pack."

"We have so many opportunities and service requests that I'm not sure which ones to pursue. Will strategic planning help us figure that out?"

"Everybody else is doing strategic planning; I guess we should too."

Not only is there considerable interest in such planning, but also confusion and skepticism—some of it well-founded. One recent study of successful innovations across thirteen industries showed that strategic planning systems often inhibit strategic thinking. Strategic planning, done poorly, can be a waste of time and may even do more harm than good.

Many of the problems nonprofit organizations have with strategic planning—confusion about how to do it, planning methods that do not fit, lack of time and money to do it—can be resolved with a dose of common sense. This workbook is a step-by-step guide for developing a strategic plan for a nonprofit organization, unit of government, service group, or association. We have found that the book is useful as:

General orientation to strategic planning

A guide for nonprofits developing a strategic plan

A tool for consultants, trainers, or corporate volunteers who assist nonprofit groups

The workbook is divided into three sections. Section I is an overview of strategic planning that tells you:

What it is

Why you should do it—and what its limitations are

How you can develop a strategic plan

Section II of the book is a step-by-step guide for developing, implementing, and updating a strategic plan. Section III includes an example of a strategic plan and blank worksheets.

What Is Strategic Planning

Strategic planning is the process of determining *what* an organization intends to be in the future and *how* it will get there (see Figure 1). It is finding the best future for your organization and the best path to reach that destination. Such planning involves fundamental choices about the future of your organization—choices about:

The mission or goals you will pursue

The programs, services, or products you will offer to accomplish this mission

How you will attract and utilize the resources you need—people, money, expertise, facilities, etc.

Figure 1: Strategic Planning

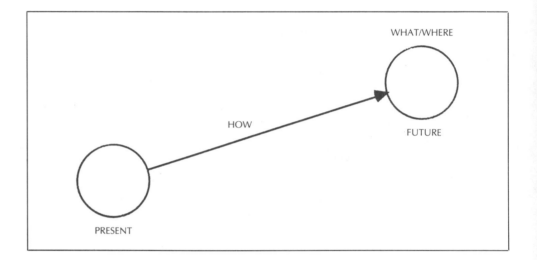

A distinction is sometimes made in planning literature between long-range planning, which focuses on what an organization intends to look like at the end of a given period of time, and strategic planning, which focuses on the action plan for how the organization will get there. In practice, however, the two go hand in hand. In this book we will use the terms strategic planning and long-range planning interchangeably to refer to the process of determining both where you want your organization to be and how you will get there.

Strategic planning is also distinguished from another kind of planning—operational or short-range planning. Operational planning is what many nonprofit organizations do when they develop yearly objectives, program plans, and budgets. Operational or short-range plans focus on a shorter time period than long-range strategic plans—for example, one year instead of five. Operational plans show in specific terms how, in the coming year, an organization will move toward the future described in its strategic plan.

Strategic planning can be described as *developing a vision* for the future of your organization. Your task in strategic planning is twofold:

Develop the best vision you can of what your organization should look like in the future, usually 2-5 years from now: its mission, services, staffing, finances, and so on.

Determine how you will move your organization toward that desired future.

Strategic planning is charting a course that you believe is wise, then adjusting that course as you gain more information and experience. A clear sense of mission and direction will guide your choices about which opportunities to pursue and which to avoid.

How does a nonprofit organization chart a course that is wise? Strategic planning can also be viewed as *finding a fit* among three sets of forces:

The mission of your organization—what you intend to accomplish

Opportunities and threats your organization faces—what is needed and feasible in your community or service area

The strengths and weaknesses of your organization—what you are capable of doing

Figure 2 on the following page depicts the fit among these forces.

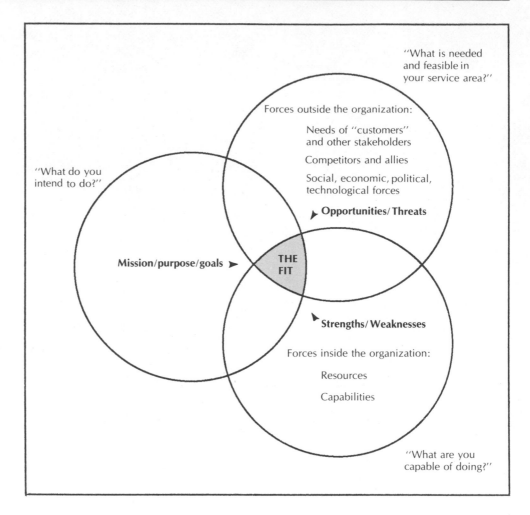

If there is not sufficient overlap between your organization's mission, its capabilities, and the needs and opportunities of your service area, then your nonprofit is in jeopardy. Effective strategic planning will help your nonprofit find the best fit among these three sets of forces. Strategic planning will help you answer the following questions: "Is our mission clear? Does our mission fit with what's needed and feasible in our service area? Does our organization have the capabilities and resources to do what's needed? If not, how will these problems be resolved?"

In summary, strategic planning is the process of determining where your organization should be in the future and how you will get there. Such planning will help an organization find the best fit for its mission, its capabilities, and its environment.

Why Develop a Strategic Plan—and the Limitations of Planning

Why should a nonprofit organization develop a plan for the future?

To improve performance

Studies have consistently shown that vision, planning, and goal-setting can positively influence organizational performance. History and great leaders have taught us that attractive visions of the future have great power. Studies also show that both large and small businesses with strategic plans outperform their counterparts without formal plans.

To stimulate forward thinking and clarify future direction

Leaders of some nonprofit organizations become so preoccupied with day-to-day issues that their organizations lose all sense of mission and direction. Strategic planning can force future thinking, highlight new opportunities and threats, and refocus an organization's mission. Strategic planning is a tool for taking control of a wandering organization. Such planning is also a way for an effective organization to stay sharp and focused.

To solve major organizational problems

Productive planning focuses on an organization's most critical problems, choices, and opportunities. Nonprofit organizations sometimes face a web of problems that are hard to address one by one. Strategic planning is a way to resolve an interrelated set of problems in an intentional, coordinated way.

To survive—even flourish—with less

The 1980s brought funding cuts and increased competition for dollars for many nonprofits. Faced with budget deficits, nonprofit organizations have several choices: increase revenue, cut expenses, put the organization together in a whole new way, deplete reserves, go into debt, or fold. Many agencies are using strategic planning to think through these tough choices.

To build teamwork and expertise

Most organizations use a team of people to develop their strategic plan. The team usually includes key staff and board members and perhaps others. People not on the planning team are also involved at key decision points. Good planning results in several benefits for participants: improved knowledge of the organization, better communication across levels and programs, improved managerial skills and an increased investment in the organization. The planning team is also a place to model the behavior and norms that you hope will persist in the future.

To influence rather than be influenced

With today's pressures, the executives and boards of nonprofits sometimes feel less like "shakers and movers" and more like "the shaken and the moved." Strategic planning can help an organization influence and control its world rather than simply respond to it.

To meet others' requirements

Some funders and regulators require organizations to have a long-range plan as a condition of funding. A strategic plan can be a good communication or marketing tool with such groups. If, however, you are developing a plan only to meet someone else's needs, don't waste more time with your planning than is absolutely necessary.

It's a natural way of doing business

Strategic planning has become a natural way of doing business for many organizations. They routinely chart and update their long- and short-term course, take action, monitor progress, then adjust actions and plans based on changing conditions. Planning becomes a familiar framework for carrying out a number of managerial responsibilities.

. . . and the Limitations

Strategic planning also has its limitations:

Costs can outweigh benefits

Strategic planning consumes time and money which might be spent more productively on other tasks. In addition, planning efforts sometimes derail: bad decisions are made, smoldering problems surface, people become enamored with the planning itself and abandon strategic thinking. Before undertaking a planning effort it is wise to ask, "Will the benefits of our planning outweigh the costs?" If costs appear to outweigh the benefits, consider whether it is wise to proceed. You may need to resolve these problems or get help before you begin.

Intuition or "muddling" may be preferable to formal planning

Some organizations are fortunate to have gifted leaders with finely developed intuition. In one sense, strategic planning can be viewed as an effort to duplicate what goes on in the mind of a gifted intuitive leader. Such leaders know well the strengths and weaknesses of their organizations; they see opportunities and threats before others do; they know instinctively the best way to proceed—sometimes without formal planning. Albert Einstein wrote:

> I believe in intuition and inspiration . . . at times I feel certain that I am right while not knowing the reason. . . . Imagination is more important than knowledge. For knowledge is limited, whereas imagination embraces the entire world, stimulating progress, giving birth to evolution.

If your organization has such a leader, you may not need to develop a formal strategic plan. Strategic planning, however, is sometimes used by such leaders as a way of sharing their vision—of bringing others along for the ride.

Other organizations prefer to muddle along without formal planning. In its best form, muddling is jumping in and responding quickly to new opportunities as they emerge. It is what a skilled football running back does in the open field. Done well, creative muddling can be an effective form of operating. Done poorly, it can kill an organization. If your organization is an effective muddler, you may want to consider whether formal strategic planning is the best way to go. An alternating pattern of formal planning and muddling is sometimes a good option for such organizations.

When ''life-threatening'' problems should be addressed first

Organizations in crisis should generally consider tackling immediate life-threatening problems before proceeding with strategic planning. For example, an organization with severe cash shortages may need to improve its cash situation to workable levels before developing a strategic plan. Hiring a new executive director may be a more pressing task than developing a strategic plan.

When implementation is unlikely

Many of us have had the experience of pouring our energy and ideas into a project that was never implemented. Disillusionment, cynicism, and feelings of powerlessness often result. If leaders have no intention of following through on plans, it may be wiser not to plan in the first place. You save time and bruised expectations. Good plans need good implementation.

When poor plans are likely

Critics of strategic planning note that some organizations develop poor plans. Faulty assumptions about the future and poor group dynamics are two reasons often cited. If you believe that your planning is or will be unproductive, we suggest that you raise that issue early, then correct the problem or get help before proceeding. One technique for reducing the risk of bad decisions is to be clear about the conditions under which you will make any major change. For example, ''We will not begin program X until we have commitments for Y dollars,'' or ''If service volume is not X by the end of next year, we will abandon the project.''

These cautions are not meant to discourage or deter you from developing plans for the future. Strategic planning can be a powerful and practical tool. Rather we are suggesting that you use strategic planning wisely.

Life-threatening problems should be addressed first

How to Develop a Strategic Plan

Research and experience strongly suggest that you use a strategic planning process that fits your organization. Nonprofits sometimes run into problems when they try to duplicate the planning methods used by another organization, often a large for-profit corporation. Planning methods that were effective in another organization may not work well for you.

Management Support Services has developed a flexible five-step model to guide nonprofit organizations in developing a strategic plan (see Figure 3).

We have found that the model can easily be adapted for either large or small nonprofit organizations. The model can also be adapted for groups that want to develop a plan quickly or those who want to use a more intensive approach. Two suggestions will help you develop a planning process that fits your organization:

Focus on Critical Issues

Focus your planning on the most critical issues that your organization faces—issues that will determine your future success or failure. Examples of critical issues are: "How will we cope with cuts in our largest source of funding?" or "How will we modify our services to meet the needs of a new target group?" Planning efforts often derail because a planning team gets bogged down in peripheral issues.

Design a Planning Process That is Realistic

Take into account such practical issues as:

Your experience with planning

If you have never developed a strategic plan, we suggest that you get some guidance from a book or article on the subject, a course or workshop, or an experienced planner.

Figure 3:
Steps to Develop a Strategic Plan

STEP 1 GET ORGANIZED	STEP 2 TAKE STOCK (SITUATION ANALYSIS)
• Decide whether to develop a strategic plan	• History and present situation
• Get commitment	• Mission
• Determine if outside help is needed	• Opportunities and threats
• Outline a planning process that fits	• Strengths and weaknesses
• Form a planning team	• Critical issues for the future

The commitment of organizational leaders

The commitment of your organization's leaders to the planning effort may be the most important key to useful planning. If you do not have this commitment, find a way to get it or do not proceed.

The time available

Don't design a planning process that will take 40 hours of meeting time when you know that 10-20 hours is as much time as you can realistically expect from staff or board. This will lead to frustration and failure. Design a planning process that you can complete realistically. Useful plans can be developed quickly.

The leadership available for the planning effort

Who will lead the planning meetings? Appoint, borrow, or hire someone who understands planning and who can guide a group through the planning process. Don't appoint someone who has no idea of what you are doing or who destroys meetings.

Technical or political problems you may encounter

Think ahead in your planning. If you anticipate difficult technical issues—like whether to develop a new "state of the art" service—how will you gain the expertise necessary to make a well-informed decision? If you anticipate political or turf problems—like getting approval from certain groups or reallocating scarce resources—consider early how these issues will be handled and when key people should get involved.

Stay focused on critical issues. Be realistic about practical issues in developing the plan. These are the keys to developing a planning process that fits your organization.

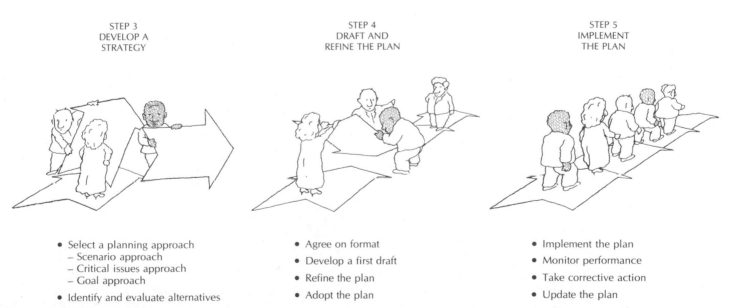

STEP 3
DEVELOP A
STRATEGY

STEP 4
DRAFT AND
REFINE THE PLAN

STEP 5
IMPLEMENT
THE PLAN

- Select a planning approach
  - Scenario approach
  - Critical issues approach
  - Goal approach
- Identify and evaluate alternatives
- Develop strategy

- Agree on format
- Develop a first draft
- Refine the plan
- Adopt the plan

- Implement the plan
- Monitor performance
- Take corrective action
- Update the plan

Six
Tips

Section II of the workbook is designed to help you develop a strategic plan step by step. As you proceed, several rules of thumb from experts across the country will be helpful:

Strategic planning is a way of thinking—an ongoing process. Your plan is never perfect or complete.

Keep the planning simple and manageable.

Involve the organizational leaders deeply. Don't give the task of planning away to support staff or a consultant.

Emphasize creativity, innovation, and imagination rather than blindly following a set of planning steps.

Don't adopt strategies without careful consideration of how they will be implemented.

Strategic planning is not an end in itself. It is simply a tool to help your organization accomplish its mission.

II

Developing Your Strategic Plan

This section is a step-by-step guide for developing a strategic plan for your organization. The pages that follow will:

Describe each of the five planning steps

Offer tips on how to accomplish each step

Provide examples that may aid you in your planning

Appendix C of this book (pages 72-88) contains blank worksheets for your planning. You may want to copy relevant sheets to use in planning team meetings. The sheets can be used as homework or completed at meetings. Worksheets can also be used to solicit information from people not on the team.

One organization's planning process will be used to illustrate this section—a community health center with a staff of fifteen. The health center was a city-sponsored program interested in becoming an independent nonprofit health center for a particular neighborhood. Use their work only as an example. Your situation may be quite different from theirs.

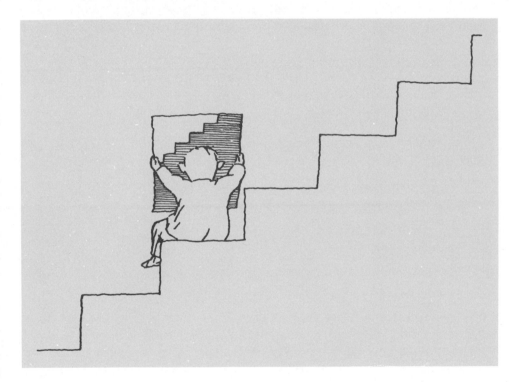

Step 1 Get Organized

- Decide whether to develop a strategic plan
- Get commitment
- Determine if outside help is needed
- Outline a planning process that fits
- Form a planning team

The major task in Step 1 is to organize your planning effort so that the time you spend will be productive. Good work in Step 1 will help your planning go smoothly in later steps. Weak groundwork in Step 1 often results in wasted time, frustration, and poor-quality plans later. In Step 1 you will:

Decide whether to develop a strategic plan

Get commitment to the planning effort

Determine if outside help is needed

Outline a planning process that fits your organization

Form a planning team

Before investing considerable effort in strategic planning, we advise you to pause for a moment to consider why you are planning and to note any concerns you have.

First consider the benefits or payoffs you anticipate from the planning. For example, do you hope that the planning will solve a growing financial problem, lead to a renewed sense of mission for your agency, or help your organization decide whether to expand? The benefits listed on pages 13–14 of this book may stimulate your thinking.

On the other hand, what are your concerns about strategic planning? For example, are you unsure how to organize the planning effort? Are you concerned that staff or board members will not devote the necessary time? Did your last attempt at strategic planning derail? Note any concerns and ways you might steer around each of them.

Weighing the possible benefits of strategic planning against any concerns, what is the wisest course of action?

Proceed with strategic planning—full steam ahead

Proceed with caution, addressing any concerns

Wait until a better time to begin

Stop—don't proceed

Complete Worksheet 1 (blank copy on page 73). List the benefits you expect from strategic planning as well as any concerns you have. Decide with other leaders of your organization how you will proceed. An example of a completed worksheet is on the following page.

Benefits and Concerns

Instructions

1) List the benefits you expect from strategic planning as well as any concerns.
2) Note possible ways to overcome each of your concerns. Circle the best ideas.
3) Decide how you will proceed.

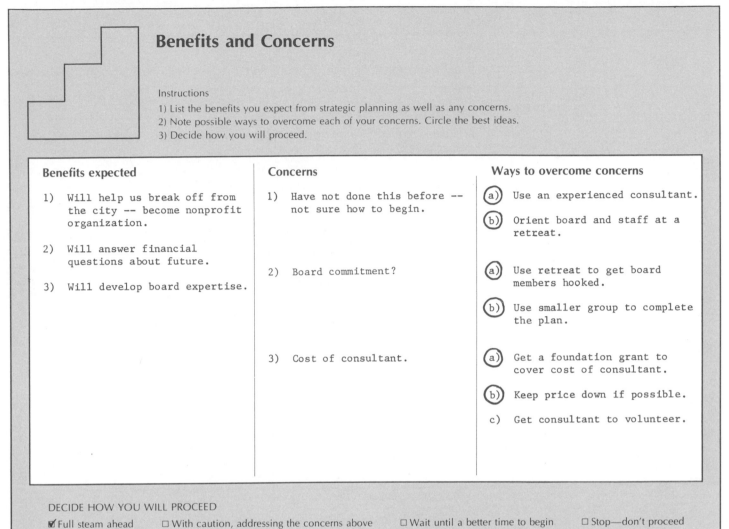

Benefits expected	Concerns	Ways to overcome concerns
1) Will help us break off from the city -- become nonprofit organization.	1) Have not done this before -- not sure how to begin.	(a) Use an experienced consultant.
		(b) Orient board and staff at a retreat.
2) Will answer financial questions about future.		
	2) Board commitment?	(a) Use retreat to get board members hooked.
3) Will develop board expertise.		(b) Use smaller group to complete the plan.
	3) Cost of consultant.	(a) Get a foundation grant to cover cost of consultant.
		(b) Keep price down if possible.
		c) Get consultant to volunteer.

DECIDE HOW YOU WILL PROCEED

☑ Full steam ahead   ☐ With caution, addressing the concerns above   ☐ Wait until a better time to begin   ☐ Stop—don't proceed

| **Get Commitment** | The commitment of an organization's leaders to planning—particularly the executive director or CEO—is critical. Don't begin without it. The commitment of board members and key staff is also important. |

When commitment is a problem, the following approaches can be effective:

Get educated

Learn more about strategic planning and how your organization can use it as a tool. A book, course, or orientation session with a consultant might help.

Discuss benefits and concerns frankly

Discuss specifically what the planning might accomplish—reduce deficits, improve services, clarify whether to merge. Clarity about payoffs can increase interest and motivation. Also discuss any concerns about the planning and how each might be addressed. The hesitant person may see a problem that others have missed.

Outline planning steps

Leaders sometimes hesitate to commit themselves to a process that is unclear or poorly conceived. Outline the steps you will use to develop the plan. Review the outline with board and key staff. Ask for suggested improvements. This can build commitment to the planning effort.

Jump in

For some, the only way to build excitement and commitment is to begin.

Build commitment to the planning effort if needed.

Determine If Outside Help is Needed

A third issue in organizing your planning is deciding whether you need help to complete the plan. Several resources are available:

> Books or articles on strategic planning
> Courses and seminars
> Consultants or advisors
> Other organizations with good planning systems

Books or articles. If you have never developed a strategic plan, a good book or article on the subject can be useful. The bibliography at the end of this book has several suggestions.

Courses and seminars. Courses, seminars, or workshops on strategic planning are available in most major cities. Check with universities, management training organizations, or professional groups. Management support organizations for nonprofit agencies exist in many cities.

Consultants or advisors. Some organizations use paid or volunteer consultants to assist with planning. A skilled consultant can help keep the planning focused and on track. A consultant or facilitator can free organizational leaders to be participants in meetings without having to manage the agenda or discussion. On the other hand, an organization can rely too heavily on a consultant so that the plan becomes the consultant's and not the organization's. Consultants sometimes cost money you do not have. Asking an experienced planner to volunteer his or her time is an option.

There are several ways consultants, facilitators, or advisors might help:

Assist in designing the planning process

Orient or train participants

Lead you through the whole process

Help you get started (to complete Steps 1 and 2 of the planning model)

Provide advice or assistance if you get stuck

Coach you from the sidelines

Provide technical advice: financial, program, other

You may need help in only one or two of the areas above. Or you may not need a consultant at all. If you do use one, be clear about what you expect. Remember that the consultant is there to serve you.

Other organizations. Another source of help is other organizations with good planning systems. Identify organizations that do good strategic planning. Find out how they do it. In addition to sharing what they do, these people might provide other assistance if asked.

Decide if you need assistance in developing your plan. If so, what kind of assistance? Get any help needed.

The primary task in organizing your planning is to outline a process that will produce a sound plan in an efficient manner. That process should be tailored to fit your organization. Section I suggested that you:

Focus the planning on the most critical issues or choices facing your organization, and

Be realistic about such practical matters as your experience with strategic planning and the time available.

The five-step model presented on pages 16 and 17 can easily be adapted to fit your organization. Strategic plans can be developed in as few as 4–6 two-hour planning meetings. Quicker can be better. Our experience shows that brief, focused planning often produces a better plan than an extended process that tends to wander. Some organizations, however, prefer to slow down their planning to allow for more data gathering, review meetings, or the development of plans across several layers of the organization.

We are often asked, "How many years should a strategic plan cover?" As a guideline we suggest that you use a period long enough to make changes in direction but not so long as to seem absurd. Generally, small nonprofits that operate in quickly changing environments plan 2-4 years into the future. A 3-5 year perspective is more common for larger organizations.

Examples of the planning processes used by two organizations follow:

Figure 4 outlines the process used by a community health center, the example used throughout this book. The center wished to develop a plan quickly.

Figure 5 is the process used by a large human service organization that developed a strategic plan for the total organization plus separate plans for each of its divisions.

**Outline a
Planning Process
That Fits Your
Organization**

*Figure 4: Strategic Planning Process
Community Health Center*

Steps	Responsible
1. Get agreement on planning steps.	Executive director Board chair Consultant
Meeting 1 *(5-hour meeting with board and key staff)*:	
2. Orient board and staff to strategic planning.	Consultant

3. Do situation analysis:
    History and present situation
    Mission
    Opportunities and threats
    Strengths and weaknesses
    Critical issues for the future
	Participants
	Consultant

4. Form board/staff team to complete the plan.	Board chair Executive director
5. Summarize situation analysis (between meetings).	Executive director Consultant
Meeting 2 *(2 hours)*:	

6. Develop scenarios for the future (scenario approach)
    Develop scenarios.
    Note areas of agreement and choices.
	Planning team
	Consultant

7. Summarize scenarios and choices (between meetings).	Executive director Consultant
8. Gather information to test feasibility of scenarios (between meetings).	Executive director
Meeting 3 *(2 hours)*:	
9. Evaluate scenarios (e.g., fit with mission, fit with needs, financial feasibility). Select the best scenario.	Planning team Consultant
10. Develop first draft of strategic plan. Include sections on mission, services, staffing, finances, facilities, and implementation (between meetings).	Executive director Consultant
Meeting 4 *(2 hours)*:	
11. Review first draft. Note suggested improvements.	Planning team Consultant
12. Revise first draft (between meetings).	Executive director Consultant
Review, adopt, and implement plan:	

13. Review second draft with
    Board
    Staff
    2-3 outsiders
    Note reactions and suggestions for improvement.
	Board chair
	Executive director
	Executive director

14. Review reactions and make needed revisions; prepare final draft.	Planning team Consultant
15. Adopt plan.	Board
16. Implement plan. Review progress every 6 months. Update plan yearly.	Executive director Board

Total meeting time, including review sessions: 18-20 hours.
Time to develop plan: 3 months.

Steps	Responsible
1. Preparation	
a. Get agreement on planning steps.	Executive director Board chair

b. Review planning process with:
   Board
   Key staff
  Make needed adjustments.
	Executive director

c. Gather information for retreat regarding:
   National, state, local trends
   Local service needs
	Executive director
	Staff
	Outside experts

2. Situation Analysis/Future Emphasis	
At a 1½-day board retreat:	

a. Do situation analysis:
   History and present situation
   Opportunities and threats
     National, state and local trends
     Service needs
     Other
   Strengths and weaknesses
   Critical issues for the future
	Board
	Executive director

b. Redefine the organization's mission and emphasis
  for the future:
   Mission
   Service emphasis
   Financial guidelines
	Board
	Executive director

c. Summarize results (after retreat).	Executive director
3. Review Sessions	
a. Review retreat summary with key staff. Get reactions and suggested revisions.	Executive director
b. Review staff comments with board. Make needed revisions in mission and emphasis statement.	Executive director
4. Division Concept Papers	

a. Develop concept papers for each division
  (twelve hours of team meetings for each division):
   Do situation analysis: mission, opportunities and threats,
    strengths and weaknesses, critical issues.
   Outline division strategy.
   Draft concept papers. Sections include division mission,
   service plans, staffing plans, financial plans.
	Division directors

b. Review division concept papers with:
   Key staff
   Board
	Executive director
	Division directors

c. Resolve critical issues across divisions (e.g., service levels, finances, etc.).	Executive director Division directors
5. Strategic Plan	

a. Draft strategic plans for:
   Total organization
   Each division (revise concept papers)
	Executive director
	Division directors

b. Review drafts of strategic plans.
  Resolve any remaining critical issues.
  Revise plans as needed.
	Executive director

c. Approve strategic plan.	Board
6. Implementation	
a. Implement plans. Review progress every 6 months.	Executive director Division directors
b. Update total organization and division plans yearly.	Board chair Executive director Division directors

Total meeting time: 60 hours.
Time to develop plan: 9 months.

Worksheet 2 will help you adapt the five-step model to fit your organization. We suggest, however, that you read the remainder of this book before completing Worksheet 2. If you are using a planning consultant, he or she can offer suggestions for organizing your planning.

Review the remainder of this book, then outline on Worksheet 2 the process you will use to develop your strategic plan. (Blank copy on pages 75 and 76.)

**Form a
Planning Team**

Most organizations use a planning team to do much of their planning. The team is usually composed of 5-8 people, but may be as small as 3 or as large as 12 or more. Generally, the larger the team, the more structure required in team meetings.

The following people could be included on the planning team:

> Full board
> Board representatives
> Executive director
> Key staff
> Other staff
> People outside the organization (people in your field, clients, funders)
> Consultants or other resource people

The composition of the team is important. It is useful to have different viewpoints represented on the team, yet to assemble a group that can function together effectively. Compose the team of people who are likely to develop the best plan. Small- to medium-sized nonprofits often use a team composed of board representatives, the executive director and key staff—with periodic reviews with the full board and the staff.

Determine who should be on the planning team. Ask those people to serve. Also decide if and how you will involve others in the planning.

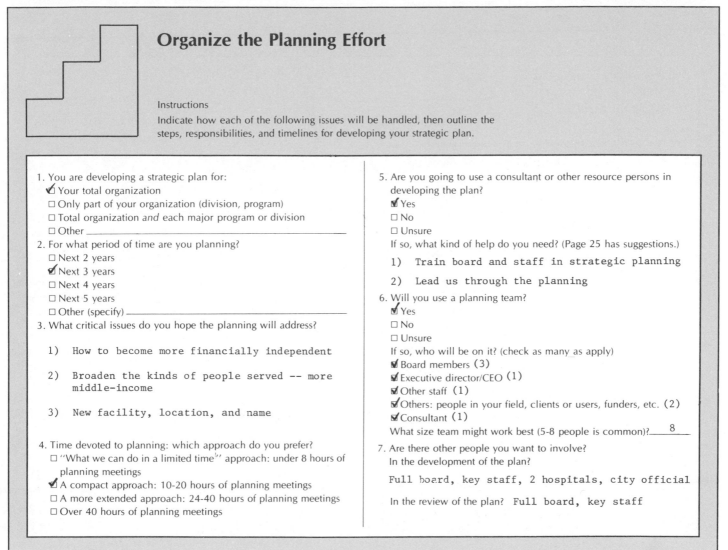

Organize the Planning Effort

Instructions

Indicate how each of the following issues will be handled, then outline the
steps, responsibilities, and timelines for developing your strategic plan.

1. You are developing a strategic plan for:
   - ☑ Your total organization
   - ☐ Only part of your organization (division, program)
   - ☐ Total organization *and* each major program or division
   - ☐ Other _____
2. For what period of time are you planning?
   - ☐ Next 2 years
   - ☑ Next 3 years
   - ☐ Next 4 years
   - ☐ Next 5 years
   - ☐ Other (specify) _____
3. What critical issues do you hope the planning will address?

   1) How to become more financially independent

   2) Broaden the kinds of people served -- more middle-income

   3) New facility, location, and name

4. Time devoted to planning: which approach do you prefer?
   - ☐ "What we can do in a limited time" approach: under 8 hours of planning meetings
   - ☑ A compact approach: 10-20 hours of planning meetings
   - ☐ A more extended approach: 24-40 hours of planning meetings
   - ☐ Over 40 hours of planning meetings

5. Are you going to use a consultant or other resource persons in developing the plan?
   - ☑ Yes
   - ☐ No
   - ☐ Unsure

   If so, what kind of help do you need? (Page 25 has suggestions.)

   1) Train board and staff in strategic planning

   2) Lead us through the planning

6. Will you use a planning team?
   - ☑ Yes
   - ☐ No
   - ☐ Unsure

   If so, who will be on it? (check as many as apply)
   - ☑ Board members (3)
   - ☑ Executive director/CEO (1)
   - ☑ Other staff (1)
   - ☑ Others: people in your field, clients or users, funders, etc. (2)
   - ☑ Consultant (1)

   What size team might work best (5-8 people is common)?___8___

7. Are there other people you want to involve?
   In the development of the plan?

   Full board, key staff, 2 hospitals, city official

   In the review of the plan? Full board, key staff

Worksheet continued on page 30

8. Who within your organization will manage the overall planning effort?

   Executive director

9. Who will lead or chair the actual planning meetings?

   Consultant and Planning Committee Chair

10. By what date do you want to have the plan approved? __October 31__

11. Outline the steps you will use in developing your plan. After outlining the process review it with the people involved, then make any changes needed.

   Steps _____ Responsible _____ By when _____

   See Figure 4

In Step 1 you have organized your strategic planning effort. You have decided to develop a strategic plan, gotten commitment from organizational leaders, enlisted any outside help needed, outlined a planning process, and formed your planning team. As you proceed you may adjust your planning process to address new issues that emerge, but the work you've done in Step 1 will help you get started and use your time wisely.

In Step 2 you will take stock of your organization's history, present situation, and future possibilities.

Step 2 Take Stock (Situation Analysis)

- History and present situation
- Mission
- Opportunities and threats
- Strengths and weaknesses
- Critical issues for the future

Your task in Step 2 is to take a hard look at your organization and the world in which you operate, then identify the issues most central to your organization's future success. In strategic planning jargon, Step 2 is often called a "situation analysis."

How do you begin? Listed below are several common areas that organizations review in taking stock of their past, present and possible future situation:

Review the organization's history and present situation

Review your mission

Assess opportunities and threats

Assess your strengths and weaknesses

Based on such review, identify the most critical issues or choices that you face regarding the future.

Time and judgment may dictate that your planning team cannot focus intensively on all of these. Some attention to each is recommended, however.

After completing Step 2 of the strategic planning process, many organizations develop a summary of their situation. Appendix A on pages 54-59 is an example of such a summary.

Each component of taking stock of your organization is described below.

Review Your Organization's History and Present Situation

History

Some planning team members may not know the history of your organization. Understanding an organization's history may be very important in charting its future.

A common method for reviewing an organization's history is for one or more people to make a presentation to the planning team covering:

The organization's beginning: start, original mission, and services, etc.

Significant events since then: major changes, successes, failures

Values that have persisted over time.

Team members can add to this account. The presentation is usually followed by a brief discussion of what values, traditions, and patterns may need to be reinforced or avoided in the future.

Present Situation

Similarly, team members may have very different views of the organization's present situation. Often, the executive of the organization will give a report to the planning team outlining the organization's present status or situation:

Current mission

Services, products, programs

Staffing

Financial position

Current plans for the future

Other important facts.

Team members then have an opportunity to ask clarifying questions and to note any issues that will need attention in the planning.

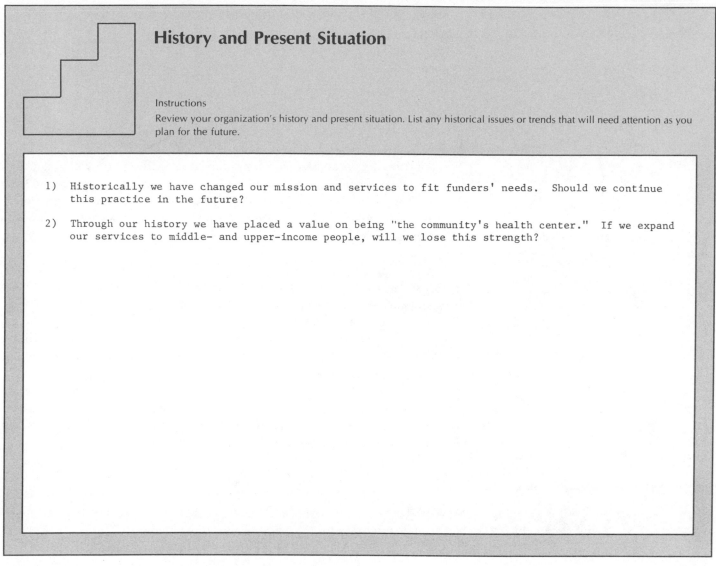

History and Present Situation

Instructions

Review your organization's history and present situation. List any historical issues or trends that will need attention as you plan for the future.

1) Historically we have changed our mission and services to fit funders' needs. Should we continue this practice in the future?

2) Through our history we have placed a value on being "the community's health center." If we expand our services to middle- and upper-income people, will we lose this strength?

Review your organization's history and present situation. List on Worksheet 3 any issues that will need attention in the next phases of planning. An example appears above.

**Review
Your
Mission**

Two fundamental strategic planning questions for nonprofit organizations are:

Is your mission clear?

Should this mission change in coming years?

Your situation analysis will now focus on these questions.

An organization's mission is a statement of its basic purpose or reason for existence. In its most simple form, the mission of a nonprofit organization describes:

What you want to achieve in the long run, and

With whom—the target group or beneficiaries of your work.

For example, the mission of a prenatal health program might be "to reduce infant mortality for low-income families in Baxter County."

Clarity about your organization's basic mission, purpose, or goal is critical to effective strategic planning. It is very difficult to chart a course for the future when you are unclear about what you intend to accomplish. Some nonprofit organizations have lost all sense of mission and direction. The programs of the agency have become ends in themselves, with little thought of the ultimate outcome or impact desired.

A good strategic plan will clearly state an organization's mission and how, in practical terms, that mission is to be accomplished. That is, what kind of services, staff, financing, etc. are most likely to produce the results you desire?

We suggest that you review your organization's present statement of mission if you have one. Your articles of incorporation should have a statement of organizational purpose or you may have another version. If none exists, attempt to get a rough mission statement on paper.

Your task in Step 2 is to review your current mission and to ask if it is the right mission for the future. Some organizations prefer to write a new statement of mission at this point in the planning. Others prefer to wait until Step 3 (Develop a Strategy) to rewrite their mission—after options for the future have been reviewed.

Use Worksheet 4 to review your organization's present mission and to note possible changes in that mission for the future. An example follows.

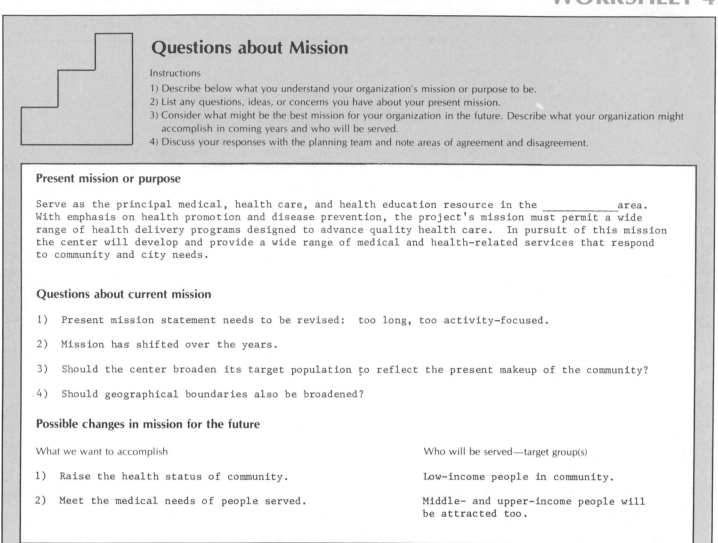

Questions about Mission

Instructions

1) Describe below what you understand your organization's mission or purpose to be.
2) List any questions, ideas, or concerns you have about your present mission.
3) Consider what might be the best mission for your organization in the future. Describe what your organization might accomplish in coming years and who will be served.
4) Discuss your responses with the planning team and note areas of agreement and disagreement.

Present mission or purpose

Serve as the principal medical, health care, and health education resource in the _____ area. With emphasis on health promotion and disease prevention, the project's mission must permit a wide range of health delivery programs designed to advance quality health care. In pursuit of this mission the center will develop and provide a wide range of medical and health-related services that respond to community and city needs.

Questions about current mission

1) Present mission statement needs to be revised: too long, too activity-focused.

2) Mission has shifted over the years.

3) Should the center broaden its target population to reflect the present makeup of the community?

4) Should geographical boundaries also be broadened?

Possible changes in mission for the future

What we want to accomplish	Who will be served—target group(s)
1) Raise the health status of community.	Low-income people in community.
2) Meet the medical needs of people served.	Middle- and upper-income people will be attracted too.

Here you will attempt to identify the major forces (present and future) from outside your organization that will make a difference in whether your nonprofit succeeds or fails. Typically you will examine:

> Customer, client, or stakeholder needs
>
> Competitors and allies
>
> Social, political, economic, and technological forces that will affect you.

Most nonprofit executives know there are forces outside the organization that influence its operation and performance. The challenge in Step 2 is to identify the most significant of those forces—called opportunities and threats—for the next several years.

This step in the planning can involve extensive data gathering from questionnaires, public meetings, interviews with key informants, focus groups, or literature review. Some organizations, however, are familiar enough with their world that they do not need to gather pounds of information about opportunities and threats. They rely primarily on the knowledge of planning team members.

The following areas are typically reviewed in identifying opportunities and threats:

Customers and other stakeholders

Research and conventional wisdom indicate that successful organizations stay close to their customers or clients. Such organizations are effective at shaping their services, programs, and products to meet client needs. In assessing opportunities and threats you will identify the needs of present and potential client groups which your organization may wish to serve in coming years. In addition to clients, others may have a stake in what you do; for example, funders, regulators, or community groups. Do these groups present opportunities or threats for the future? Your analysis in Step 2 will identify the most critical of these opportunities and threats.

Competitors and allies

Virtually every nonprofit competes for something; for example, funding, clients, or the public's attention. Your analysis of opportunities and threats will also focus on your competitive situation. Generally speaking, are you strong or vulnerable in relation to your competitors?

Nonprofits in highly competitive fields may wish to spend more time in Step 2 on questions like:

> With whom do we compete?
>
> For what do we compete?
>
> What are our relative competitive strengths or weaknesses—cost, quality, image, etc.?

One nonprofit that was heavily dependent on income for its recreational programs was virtually put out of business when a much more attractive recreation facility was built down the street by an organization competing for the same clientele. Are there major opportunities or threats that your organization faces from its competitors?

On the other hand, all organizations need not be considered adversaries or threats. Many nonprofits team up with other organizations in order to better accomplish their missions. A human service organization working with disabled people might team up with an employment program so that both organizations, and ultimately the disabled people themselves, will benefit. Are there major opportunities for your organization in teaming up with other organizations?

Virtually every nonprofit competes for something

Social, political, economic and technological forces

Opportunities and threats also come from the following areas:

Social or cultural—changing demographics, societal or cultural trends

Political—new legislation, changes in leadership, political support

Economic—changes in funding patterns, economic trends

Technological—general technology (computers, telecommunications, etc.), new developments or practices in your field

Are there major opportunities and threats from these areas that you should consider in charting your organization's course for the future?

Use Worksheet 5 (an example appears below) to identify the major opportunities and threats your organization faces for the future. A 2- to 5-year perspective is often used. Worksheets 5a and b (Appendix C) are available if you wish to focus in more detail on the needs of your customers or on your competition. Complete Worksheet 5, then select the 4–8 most critical opportunities or threats you will need to consider in developing plans for the future.

WORKSHEET 5

Opportunities and Threats

Instructions

1) List the major opportunities (O) and threats (T) that you believe your organization will face in the next 2-5 years that will determine whether it succeeds or fails.

2) Worksheets 5a and b may be useful if you wish to do a more detailed analysis of your customers or competition.

3) Combine your responses with those of other planning team members, then identify the 4-8 opportunities or threats that are most critical to your organization's future success.

Clients, customers, stakeholders	Competitors and allies	Social, cultural, economic, political, or technological forces
Basic health care needs in the community are not being met -- is a strong need for our services (O)	Competition from HMO's could reduce number who use the center (T) No formal affiliation with hospital -- could hurt continuity of care (O/T) Have many supporters (federal, state, local) -- can use this support when become independent (O)	Part of our federal funding may be cut (T) Possible changes in Medicare and Medicaid: - Mandatory HMO -- could lose present patients (T) - Cuts/freezes in benefits -- financial pressures (T) - Pressure for more outpatient care (O)

**Assess the
Strengths and Weaknesses
of Your Organization**

An organization's resources and capabilities—or lack thereof—are also critical in creating a viable future. The world may present a wide array of opportunities and threats, but is your organization capable of responding to those? Will you have sufficient staff, expertise, money, and other resources to create the future you desire for your organization? Or does your organization have resources or capabilities that should be better utilized?

A problem with capabilities

An old, established human service organization had grown stale and unresponsive. Led by a new executive director, the organization identified a number of pressing community needs that fit within the agency's mission. A major problem was also identified: the agency's staff did not appear capable of meeting the new needs.

What should the agency do? Options included: hire new staff in addition to old, replace existing staff with new people, retrain existing staff, redesign jobs to fit skills, do not pursue the new needs. After carefully examining each option, the agency's leaders decided on the following approach:

> Pursue the new needs
>
> Fire some staff—with generous outplacement and severance benefits
>
> Hire new staff to replace them
>
> Redesign some jobs
>
> Retrain the remaining staff

Within eighteen months the agency made these changes as humanely as possible and was successful in meeting the new needs.

Part of your strategic planning will focus on whether your organization has the resources and capabilities to achieve its mission.

A knowledge of your strengths will help you keep focused and see new opportunities for service. A candid assessment of weaknesses will inject a dose of realism in your planning.

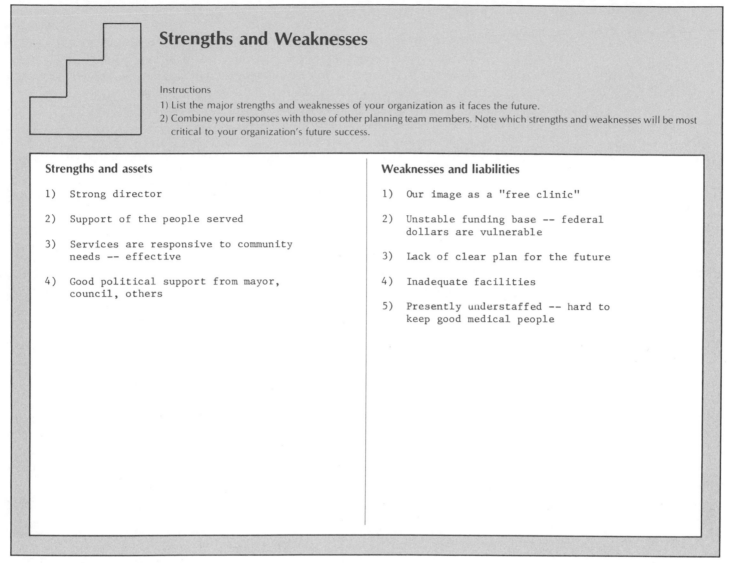

Strengths and Weaknesses

Instructions

1) List the major strengths and weaknesses of your organization as it faces the future.

2) Combine your responses with those of other planning team members. Note which strengths and weaknesses will be most critical to your organization's future success.

Strengths and assets

1) Strong director

2) Support of the people served

3) Services are responsive to community needs -- effective

4) Good political support from mayor, council, others

Weaknesses and liabilities

1) Our image as a "free clinic"

2) Unstable funding base -- federal dollars are vulnerable

3) Lack of clear plan for the future

4) Inadequate facilities

5) Presently understaffed -- hard to keep good medical people

Use Worksheet 6 (an example appears above) to assess the strengths and weaknesses of your organization. After completing Worksheet 6, identify what you believe to be the 3–4 most important strengths and weaknesses that you will need to consider in planning for the future.

**Summarize the
Critical Issues
for the Future**

Your final task in taking stock is to summarize the critical issues that your organization faces concerning its future. In identifying these issues you will draw upon all the work you have just completed in Step 2.

Although your organization may face many important issues or choices, we suggest that you try to identify the 4-8 issues most crucial to your nonprofit's future success. It may be helpful to state each issue in the form of a question that can be answered. For example, you might state a financial issue as follows: "How can projected deficits in each of the next three years be avoided?"

In Step 3 (Develop a Strategy) you will answer these questions.

Use Worksheet 7 to list what you believe to be the most critical issues facing your organization over the next 2–5 years. An example of one organization's issues is on the facing page.

After completing Step 2 (Take Stock) summarize your findings and review them with the planning team, board, staff, or appropriate others to ensure that your conclusions are accurate and complete. Make any additions or changes needed. Appendix A is an example of one organization's situation analysis.

**Step 2
Summary**

In Step 2 you have reviewed the history, present situation and possible future of your organization. You have looked both inside your organization—and at the world in which you operate. You have summarized your findings and developed a manageable list of 4-8 critical issues which you will need to address in your next phase of planning. You are now ready to develop a strategy for the future (Step 3).

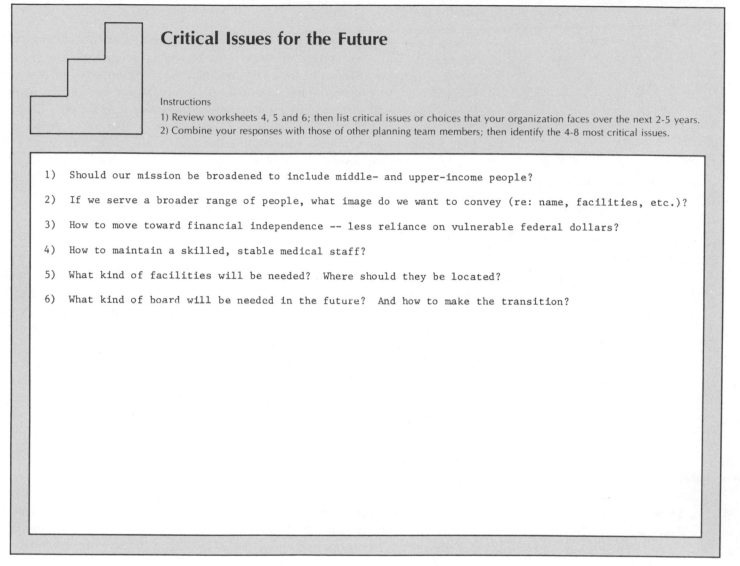

Critical Issues for the Future

Instructions

1) Review worksheets 4, 5 and 6; then list critical issues or choices that your organization faces over the next 2-5 years.
2) Combine your responses with those of other planning team members; then identify the 4-8 most critical issues.

1) Should our mission be broadened to include middle- and upper-income people?

2) If we serve a broader range of people, what image do we want to convey (re: name, facilities, etc.)?

3) How to move toward financial independence -- less reliance on vulnerable federal dollars?

4) How to maintain a skilled, stable medical staff?

5) What kind of facilities will be needed? Where should they be located?

6) What kind of board will be needed in the future? And how to make the transition?

Step 3 Develop a Strategy

- Select a planning approach
  - Scenario approach
  - Critical issues approach
  - Goal approach
- Identify and evaluate alternatives
- Develop strategy

In Step 2 you identified a number of opportunities and choices for your organization. Your task in Step 3 is to sort through those choices and formulate a realistic strategy for the future. You will describe the kind of organization you want to be and how you will make the transition from the present to that future. By the end of Step 3 your organization's strategy should be clear enough to draft your strategic plan.

In Step 3 you will select a planning approach that will enable you to identify and evaluate alternative futures for your organization and develop an overall strategy for moving toward the desired future.

We have found that there are three basic methods or approaches for formulating an organization's strategy for the future:

Scenario approach

Critical issues approach

Goal approach

These approaches may be used individually or in combination. We recommend, however, that you begin Step 3 by selecting one of the approaches around which to organize your planning. For example, the planning team may decide that the scenario approach is the most productive way to proceed, so in Step 3 the team would begin with that approach. Or the team may decide that the critical issues or a goal approach is a more productive way to begin.

Most texts on strategic planning, written primarily for large for-profit corporations, suggest the goal approach. Our experience has been that many nonprofits, particularly small-to-medium-sized agencies, find the scenario or critical issues approach a more productive way to begin Step 3. Goals can be set later in the planning. More will be said about this later.

Each approach is described below.

Scenario Approach

With the scenario approach you develop several alternative pictures of what your organization might look like in the future. You then pick the best scenario and refine it.

Begin by outlining one or more pictures of the future. For example, the community health center, mentioned previously, used the scenario approach to begin Step 3 of its planning. The planning team began Step 3 with a two-hour meeting. After reviewing a summary of work done in Step 2, each team member took about ten minutes to describe the best possible future that he or she could imagine for the Center. Team members were given the following special instructions:

> "Imagine that it is three years from now and your organization has been put together in a very exciting way. Imagine that you are a newspaper reporter who is doing a story on the organization at that time. You have thoroughly reviewed the center's mission, services, personnel, finances, relationships, etc. Describe in a few phrases or a picture what it is that you see."

After making their notes, each planning team member shared his or her vision for the future. The meeting leader recorded the components of each person's vision. At the end of the meeting, the similarities and differences among visions were listed and discussed. Several basic options were identified:

Continue as a division of the city health department.

Break off from the city. Become an independent community health clinic with ties to hospitals and other clinics.

Become a community health and human service center that houses our organization and several other agencies serving the same target population.

Become a component of a consolidated medical program, similar to a HMO, that offers basic health services as well as several specialized services. Participating health centers would provide other specialties.

After the meeting the executive director talked with several other organizations to determine if there might be interest in the last two options.

At a second two-hour planning team meeting the executive director reported her findings. Team members rated each scenario on several factors (fit with mission, fit with community needs, financial feasibility), then listed the relative advantages and disadvantages of each scenario. By the end of the meeting the strategy that looked most promising was a combination of the options first identified:

Break off from the city. Become an independent community health center, housed in our own building. Establish a new and clearer identity. Expand our target group to include middle-income people—also expand our service area. Improve staffing ratios. Ask 2-3 other organizations with complementary services (mental health, financial counseling, and perhaps day care) to have offices in the building. Develop and maintain ties with 2-3 hospitals and 3-4 community health clinics. Negotiate reimbursement from at least 3 HMOs.

The planning team discussed this scenario with board and staff between team meetings and received authorization from the board to further test whether this scenario was feasible.

At a third planning team meeting, the team identified areas needing more investigation, then resolved as many questions as possible in the time remaining. After the third meeting the executive director translated the preferred scenario into the first draft of a strategic plan (see Appendix B). The draft was reviewed with the full board, staff, and two knowledgeable people outside the organization. The plan was refined, then approved by the board.

This, in essence, is the scenario approach for developing a strategic plan. The approach has the following advantages:

It is quick

It holds people's interest

It uses "big picture" thinking—it is useful in thinking about major shifts in emphasis or direction

Develop a vision of the future

Steps in the scenario approach.

In summary, the scenario approach includes the following four steps:

Identify major scenarios for the future

Evaluate scenarios

Select the preferred scenario

Test and refine it

A second method of developing your vision or strategy for the future is the critical issues approach.

Using this approach, the planning team will sequence critical issues from Step 2 in some logical order. Each issue is then resolved in turn. Possible solutions to each issue are listed and the best solution chosen. Prior decisions are sometimes revised in light of later decisions. After resolving major issues, the planning team reviews the organization's overall strategy to ensure that it is sound.

A chemical dependency treatment program identified the following critical issues in Step 2 of its planning:

Services

Should we modify our services? If so, how?

> Emphasize residential or outpatient services
>
> Begin services to seniors
>
> Expand intermediate care facilities for adolescents and women
>
> Centralize or expand the family program
>
> Start a DWI program
>
> Expand technical assistance services

Should we go after national markets more aggressively? If so, how?

Finances

How can we avoid recurring cash shortages?

If county funding for the outpatient program is cut, what should be done?

How would expansion into other states be financed?

Administration

Should program directors be held more accountable for program performance, including financial performance?

What functions should be computerized?

The planning team then decided to address the issues in the following order:

1. *Services*	2. *Finances*	3. *Administration*
Modify services?	How to avoid cash shortages?	Program director responsibilities?
National markets?	What to do with outpatient program?	Computerization?
	How to finance expansion?	

A series of six two-hour planning team meetings was used to list the options for resolving each issue, then to pick the best option. For example, in deciding whether or not to pursue national markets, the planning team listed the following options (the preferred options are noted*).

Should we go after national markets more aggressively?

Options:

> Do not pursue national markets.
>
> *Aggressively recruit out-of-state clients for our present residential programs.

* Test the feasibility of one residential center—through a joint venture with another organization over the next two years. They supply the start-up capital; we supply the expertise.

Yes, develop residential programs in 2–3 major cities over the next four years. Expand further, if feasible.

During a later meeting the planning team considered *How to avoid recurring cash shortages* and listed these options.

Options:

* Cut costs further.

* Tighten procedures for predicting and monitoring cash flow.

Generate more non-fee revenue (grants, fundraising, etc.).

Continue only profitable programs.

* Generate cash surpluses through residential programs.

* Develop a realistic three-year financial plan for any new or expanded program.

* More aggressively collect accounts receivable.

* Prioritize accounts payable. Pay in that order.

* Build cash reserves to workable levels (20% of budget).

The agency's strategy for the future became more clear as each issue was answered. After all issues were addressed, the planning team met to review the soundness of the agency's overall strategy for the future. They asked questions like, "Are our service plans consistent with financial plans?" and "Is staffing adequate to accomplish the service plans?"

After the six meetings the executive director completed a first draft of a four-year plan for the agency using much the same format as Appendix B. The planning team, board, and staff reviewed the draft, which was then revised and adopted.

Steps in the Critical Issues Approach

Sequence the issues

Resolve each issue

Check to see that you have developed a clear, sound strategy for the organization

The goal approach

Goal Approach

A third way to begin Step 3 is to set several major goals or targets for the organization in coming years, then determine the best strategy to reach each goal.

The goal approach is often used by for-profit corporations that focus on a few major goals or targets that drive the organization—for example, profitability or market share. Goals are set for these areas, strategies are developed to reach each goal, and more detailed plans of work are formulated for accomplishing each strategy.

Some nonprofit organizations have difficulty using the goal approach early in Step 3 because their goals are not yet clear. You may prefer to begin Step 3 with the scenario or critical issues approach, then set specific goals for the organization later in Step 3, after your strategy for the future becomes clearer.

Larger nonprofit organizations sometimes use the goal approach to set overall emphasis or direction for the organization. Divisions, units, or programs of the organization then incorporate those goals in their strategic plans. For example, one large nonprofit began its planning in Step 3 by setting four major goals for the future:

Increase services to people living below the poverty level.

Increase quality of service.

Increase contract and fee income.

Automate as feasible (program, billing, and personnel records).

Each major program or staff unit in the organization then developed specific objectives and work plans outlining how these goals would be met. The program objectives and work plans were incorporated into the first draft of the agency's strategic plan.

Steps in the Goal Approach

Set goals

Identify possible strategies or objectives to reach each goal

Select the best strategies

Outline specific plans to accomplish each strategy

Decide which planning approach to use in Step 3 (scenario, critical issues, goal or some combination). Then use this approach to determine what your organization should look like in the future and how you will get there.

Common Strategies for Nonprofits

In planning with large numbers of nonprofit organizations, our staff have noticed these frequently mentioned strategies:

Grow: become large and powerful, diversify services and funding sources

Team up: merge, consolidate, develop joint programming, or share services with other nonprofits

Downsize: reduce the scope of services to fit financial or other constraints

Focus or specialize: do a few things very well, find a niche

Become entrepreneurial: earn income to offset declining revenue or to subsidize other services

Obtain government contracts: provide services mandated by government agencies

Professionalize: increase staff skills and credentials

Deprofessionalize: provide services using mutual help, social supports, client-to-client methods, or volunteers

Go out of business: call it quits if your organization is no longer viable or has fulfilled its mission

Step 3 Summary

In Step 3 you have selected a method for identifying and evaluating strategies for the future: scenario approach, critical issues approach, goal approach, or some combination. Using this approach you have developed a realistic picture of what your organization will be as well as the best path for moving towards that future.

In Step 4 you will draft and refine your strategic plan.

The bibliography at the end of the text lists a number of books, articles, and journals that may be useful in developing strategy or solving problems for your organization.

Your major tasks in Step 4 are to get a first draft of the plan on paper, refine it, then adopt the plan.

Common activities in Step 4 include:

Agree on a format for the plan

Develop a first draft

Refine the plan

Adopt the plan.

We strongly suggest that your planning team agree on a format for your plan before someone attempts a first draft. We often encourage our clients to agree early (Step 1) on a rough outline of what the plan might look like because planning team members may have very different images of what a strategic plan is.

The critical issues addressed in your plan should influence the format of the plan. For example, if one of the major issues facing your organization is whether to erect a new building, you will probably have a section in your plan that addresses facilities. If your facilities are not a major issue, you will not need such a section. Figure 6 and Appendix B contain a format for strategic plans that many nonprofit organizations have found useful.

- Agree on format
- Develop a first draft
- Refine the plan
- Adopt the plan

Develop a format for your strategic plan if you have not already done so. Outline what your strategic plan will look like.

Section headings usually include:

Mission and Strategy

A statement of your organization's mission and a summary of your strategy for accomplishing that mission. This section serves as an executive summary for the rest of the plan.

Service Plans

A description of programs, services, or products over the planning period (including new services) and projections of service levels for each year of the plan.

1. Service description

Program/service/product	Goal	Target group	Target area

2. Levels of service

Program/service/product	Units of service	Base year(s)	Year 1	Year 2	Year 3	Year 4	Year 5

Figure 6: Format for Strategic Plans

Continued

Figure 6 continued

Staffing Plans
A summary of the staff and volunteers needed.

		Full-time equivalents				
Positions	Base year(s)	Year 1	Year 2	Year 3	Year 4	Year 5

Financial Plans
An operating budget for each year of the plan. Other financial sections may be needed if large capital purchases are planned (land, buildings, equipment) or large amounts of funds are to be raised for other than operating purposes (e.g., an endowment). Include amount needed and sources of revenue for such items.

	Base year(s)	Year 1	Year 2	Year 3	Year 4	Year 5
1. Operating budget						
Revenue (by source):						
Expense (by line item or program):						
Surplus/(deficit)						
2. Other						

Implementation plan
Major tasks or objectives to be accomplished to implement the plan.

Tasks/objectives	Responsible	By when

Section headings sometimes include:

Needs, problems, goals: Description of major needs or problems to be addressed or goals to be achieved.

Target population, groups: Description of groups to be served.

Organization, structure: Organization chart or description of the organizational structure planned for the future.

Facilities plan: Plans for building or physical plant.

Governance: Description of plans for Board of Directors or membership.

Marketing: Marketing plans: target population, services or products, pricing, promotion, etc.

Key relationships: Important relationships and how each will be developed or maintained.

Policies: Organizational policies for the future (re: programming, finances, other).

Assumptions: Assumptions upon which the plan is based. You may want to list assumptions for each section of the plan.

Risks, contingency plans: A description of risks associated with the plan or back-up plans to be pursued if circumstances change.

Other: Issues not adequately addressed above.

Develop a first draft of your strategic plan using an agreed-upon format.

**Develop a
First Draft**

After your strategy for the future is relatively clear (from Step 3), one or more planning team members should develop a first draft of your strategic plan. A common response we hear at this point is: "Our organization is not clear enough about our plans to develop a first draft." We encourage you to attempt a first draft anyway. Appendix B is an example of what your first draft might look like.

It is difficult for more than two or three people to develop a draft of anything. We suggest that one or two planning team members develop the first draft of your plan, which can then be reviewed with the full team and others.

It is quite common for new critical issues to emerge as the first draft of your plan is being developed or reviewed. For example, your financial strategies may not look sound when you attempt to develop three-year budgets. Don't be overly concerned if your first draft is not perfect. The draft will be improved and revised through the review process which follows.

We strongly suggest that your strategic plan include a section outlining how you will implement the plan. Identify the major tasks or objectives that need to be accomplished, who is responsible for each task and timelines. Appendix B contains an example of a relatively simple implementation plan (page 71).

Some organizations develop an implementation plan as part of the first or second draft. Others wait until the plan is in more final form. A good implementation plan is often a test of whether the goals outlined in the strategic plan are realistic.

**Refine
the Plan**

In Step 1 (Get Organized) we suggested that you consider people or groups with whom you might like to review the plan. If you have not decided who needs to review the plan and how it will be reviewed, do so now.

Drafts of the plan are commonly reviewed with:

Planning team

Staff

Board or other decision-makers

Interested people outside the organization who have a stake in your future

An agenda for review meetings that often works well is:

Overview of the plan

What is your general reaction to the plan? Is it in the ballpark?

What specifically do you like about each section of the plan?

What problems, soft spots or omissions do you see in each section?

What specific suggestions do you have about how the plan can be strengthened or improved?

Next steps to complete the plan

*What soft spots
do you see?*

When your plan is near its final form, we also suggest you ask:

Where is there risk in this plan?

Do you want to live with this level of risk or should you do something to reduce the risk?

Your task in the reviews is to develop a plan that is both sound and implementable—and one that people understand and will carry out. Remember that you will never have a perfect plan. Your organization will change continually as will conditions in the world around you. As you act on your plan you will get new information which may require adjustments in your vision of the future or in your plan for getting there.

Review your plans with appropriate people and groups, then make needed revisions.

Adopt the Plan

We recommend that your strategic plan be reviewed and approved by appropriate decision-makers in the organization. In most nonprofit organizations, the board of directors reviews and approves the strategic plan. In other organizations the executive or other staff may need to give approval.

Get approval of your strategic plan as needed. Then celebrate!

Step 4 Summary

In Step 4 you have developed a first draft of your strategic plan. You have refined or improved your plan through reviews with appropriate people. You have adopted the plan. In Step 5 you will begin to implement the plan and update it as needed.

Step 5 Implement the Plan

A common misconception is: When your strategic plan is adopted, your planning is complete. A better view is: When your plan is adopted, a new phase of planning has begun.

Remember that implementing the plan, monitoring progress, making midcourse corrections and updating your plan are all part of the strategic planning process.

Make sure that the directions and strategies in your strategic plan are incorporated into the coming year's objectives and budget. Then act. A good plan needs good implementation. Review progress toward the plan at six- or twelve-month intervals. Ask:

Are we meeting our goals? If not, why not?

Are our vision and strategy for the future still sound? If not, what changes are needed?

- Implement the plan
- Monitor performance
- Take corrective action
- Update the plan

Then take corrective action or change the plan, as needed.

Most organizations update their strategic plans yearly, before they plan and budget for the coming year. A common method for yearly updates of the plan is:

Reassess opportunities and threats, strengths and weaknesses, and critical issues using the worksheets. Has anything new emerged?

Review your strategy for the future. Is it still sound?

Revise the plan including service, staffing and financial projections, and the implementation plan.

Review the revised plan with board, staff, and any appropriate others. Get approval of major changes.

Translate the revised strategic plan into the coming year's program goals, budgets, etc. (operational planning).

Section Summary

Using the steps outlined in this workbook you have developed a picture of where you want your organization to be at some future time and outlined the best path to reach that destination. You will take action based upon your strategic plan, then adjust your plan with experience.

Remember that strategic planning is not an end in itself, but a tool to better accomplish your organization's mission. We hope that those you serve will be the ultimate beneficiaries of your planning.

Bibliography

Books

Robert J. Allio and Malcolm W. Pennington, eds., *Corporate Planning: Techniques and Applications*. AMACOM, New York, 1979.

Kenneth R. Andrews, *The Concept of Corporate Strategy*. Dow Jones-Irwin, Homewood, Illinois, 1980.

*James M. Hardy, Ph.D., *Managing for Impact in Nonprofit Organizations: Corporate Planning Techniques and Applications*. Essex Press, Erwin, Tennessee, 1984.

*Philip Kotler, *Marketing for Nonprofit Organizations*. Prentice-Hall, Inc., Englewood Cliffs, New Jersey, 1982.

Stephanie K. Marrus, *Building the Strategic Plan: Find, Analyze and Present the Right Information*. John Wiley & Sons, New York, 1984.

Thomas H. Naylor, *Corporate Planning Models*. Addison-Wesley, Reading, Massachusetts, 1979.

Michael Porter, *Competitive Advantage: Creating and Sustaining Superior Performance*. The Free Press, New York, 1985.

Michael E. Porter, *Competitive Strategy: Techniques for Analyzing Business, Industry and Competitors*. The Free Press, New York, 1980.

Alan J. Rowe, Richard O. Mason, and Karl Dickel, *Strategic Management and Business Policy: A Methodological Approach*. Addison-Wesley, Reading, Massachusetts, 1982.

George A. Steiner, *Strategic Planning: What Every Manager Must Know*. The Free Press, New York, 1979.

Noel M. Tichy, *Managing Strategic Change, Technical, Political and Cultural Dynamics*. John Wiley & Sons, New York, 1983.

Benjamin B. Tregoe and John W. Zimmerman, *Top Management Strategy: What It Is and How to Make It Work*. Simon & Schuster, New York, 1980.

*United Way of America, *Scenarios: A Tool for Planning in Uncertain Times* (1984), *Strategic Management and United Way* (1986), *What Lies Ahead: A Mid-Decade View* (1985). Alexandria, Virginia.

Journals

Harvard Business Review. Harvard University, Boston.

Journal of Business Strategy. Warren, Gorham & Lamont, Boston.

Long Range Planning. Pergamon Press for the Society for Long Range Planning, Elmsford, New York.

Planning Review. Robert J. Allio & Associates, Inc. for the North American Society for Corporate Planning, Duxbury, Massachusetts.

Strategic Management Journal. John Wiley & Sons, New York.

*Materials geared specifically to nonprofit organizations.

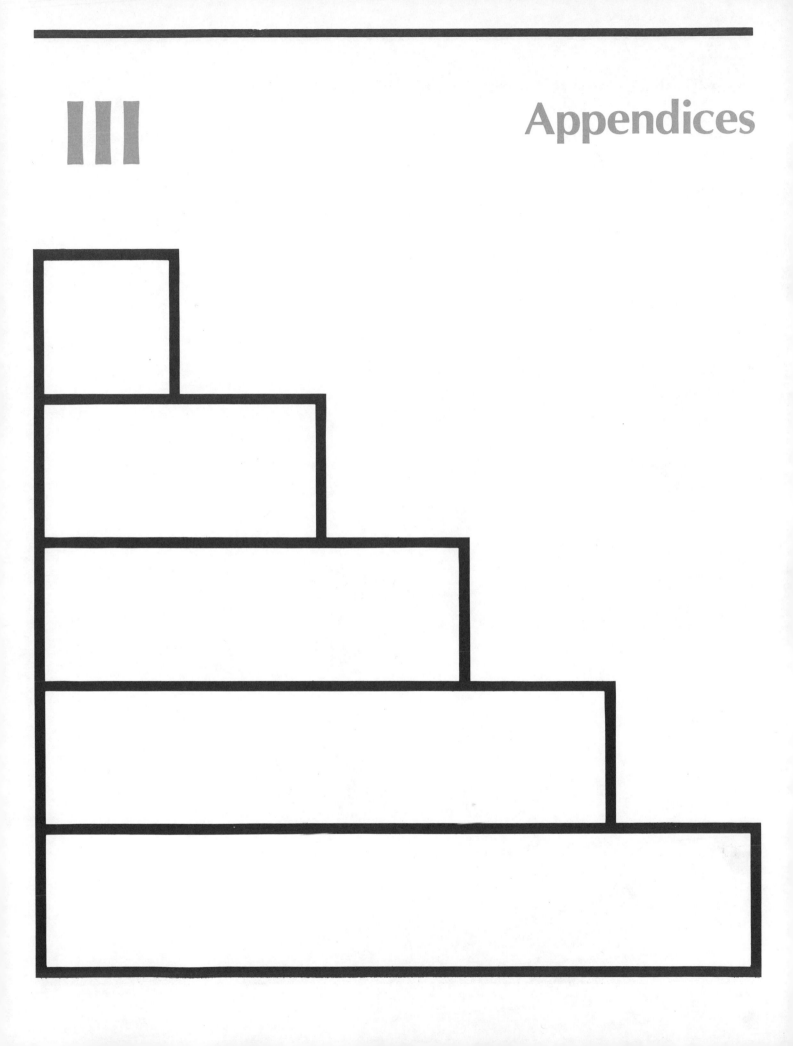

Appendices

Appendix A: Summary of a Situation Analysis

COMMUNITY HEALTH CENTER
SUMMARY OF SITUATION ANALYSIS

HISTORY

1. Center began as a Model Cities program - lots of money. Mission was to provide health services to the community.

2. Primary funding shifted to other services (UHI, MA State grants, fees). Mission changed to raising the health status of the community - more emphasis on preventive health care. Became tied more closly to the City's Health Department.

3. Now engaged in negotiations with the City to become a free-standing nonprofit organization.

THEMES

1. Serve the community
2. Shape mission and services to fit funding

Comment: These two themes could conflict

VALUES

1. We are "the community's health center": responsive to needs, Board and staff are representative of community.
2. Quality services

COMMENTS AND QUESTIONS ABOUT THE CENTER'S MISSION

1. The Center's general statement of mission has changed over the years:

    *   From providing health services to the community to
    *   Raising the health status of the community to
    *   Present "Statement of Mission and Goals"

2. The present "Statement of Mission and Goals" may not be a good statement for the future - too long and too focused on activities (vs. results).

3. To what extent should funding concerns influence the Center's mission?

4. Who should the Center's target population be?

    *   Present clientele (mainly low income)
    *   Whoever lives in the community (include middle and upper income)
    *   Other: focus on women and their children

5. Should the Center broaden its geographical service area? If so, what should that area be?

6. Should the Center's mission be stated in terms that are achievable?

OPPORTUNITIES (O) AND THREATS (T)

Votes
n=14

7   1. Competition from HMOs may reduce the number of people who use the
        Center. Some people who might like to use the Center may not be
        able to. (T)

6   2. There is a market for our services. We are in a medically
        underserved area. (O)

6   3. Federal funds for programs like ours may be cut. (T)

6   4. The Center is not meeting several federal indicators (pharmacy and
        physician/client ratio). This could affect funding. (T)

6   5. Changes in Medicare and Medicaid may:

        • Force people into HMOs (T)
        • Cut or freeze benefits (T)
        • Move health services into more outpatient care (O)

6   6. Lack of full and formal affiliation with a hospital may hurt
        continuity of service. (T)

6   7. The Center has many allies: (O)

        • Federal (grants management staff)
        • State (Health Department)
        • Metro (Metropolitan Health Planning Board)
        • Local (Community Services, Mayor)

4   8. The Center could become part of a new consolidated medical program
        (CMP). (O/T)

3   9. Changes on the block we want to move to:

        • Make that street a good place to move to (O)
        • Necessitate changes in our image (O/T)

3   10. The "feminization of poverty" will mean that there will be more
        women with children under 6 in need of child care. Perhaps the
        Center should provide such child care. (O)

3   11. There is an opportunity for the Center to get into community-based
        education and continuing education through the public schools,
        University, etc. (O)

3   12. There will be more senior citizens in the community in need of
        health care in coming years. (O)

3   13. The Center lacks support from the medical and dental community.
         (T)

1   14. The Center needs to be able to shift its services to meet epidemic
         shifts (e.g. AIDS, herpes, etc.). (O/T)

1   15. The Center could tailor its services to the needs of the minority
         populations it serves. (O)

1   16. The Center could conduct continuing education events for health
         care professionals. (O)

1   17. With growing depersonalization in the health care field, the
         Center can provide personalized care -- e.g. people are able to
         get the same doctor here. (O)

1   18. The Center needs more funders as allies. (O)

1   19. There is potential for increased/new money from the city and
         county -- similar to funds received for other community clinics.
         (O)

STRENGTHS AND WEAKNESSES

Strengths	Weaknesses

Votes n=14		Votes n=14	
11	1. Strong director	12	1. Image: "free clinic"
10	2. Support of the people served	10	2. Unstable funding -- reliance on federal dollars that may not be there in the future
10	3. Good political support (mayor, council, etc.)	8	3. Lack of a plan for the future
10	4. Length of service in the community -- range of services, responsive, how service is delivered	7	4. Inadequate facility: not enough space, appearance, distractions, lights, etc.
9	5. Key staff	7	5. More promotion and marketing needs to be done
6	6. Board represents a good mixture or cross-section of people	7	6. City control: personnel issues, contracts, political risks
5	7. We have "a franchise" to serve our area	6	7. Staff shortage; Only 1 doctor --discontinuity of medical care, clerical turnover
5	8. Some funding sources are stable	6	8. Collection of patient revenues
4	9. Dedication and creativity of staff and board	5	9. Relative newness of the Board as a governing body -- complexity of the issues
4	10. Good medical people on staff and board	5	10. Location
4	11. Some staff have a lot of potential to be developed	5	11. Name
3	12. Good Board chair	4	12. Lack a good management information system
2	13. Location -- been there a long time	3	13. Hours of services -- no night hours (have some now)
		2	14. Staff development, training and motivation

CRITICAL ISSUES FOR THE FUTURE

Votes
n=14

10 1. Community Support

• How can the Center develop and maintain support from:
- Neighborhood
- Political and funding communities
- Medical community

10 2. Mission and Target Population

• Should the Center expand its services to middle and upper income people? If so, how will they be attracted?
• Should our geographic service area be expanded?

7 3. Staff

• How can the Center maintain a skilled, stable medical staff?

5 4. Board

• What kind of Board will be needed in the future?
• What will be the Board's role (vs staff's role) in leading the agency?

5 5. Funding

• How can the Center move from position of financial dependence to independence?

- 6. Image

• What is the image that the Center wishes to convey to the community? How will it be conveyed? (eg. name, facility, etc.)

- 7. Facility

• Should the Center move out of its present facility to its own building? If so, where should the building be located? How should it be financed?

Appendix B: Example of a Strategic Plan

COMMUNITY HEALTH CENTER
THREE YEAR PLAN

MISSION AND STRATEGY

The mission of Community Health Center is to improve the health status of residents in the _____ community. Over the next three years the Center will provide affordable primary medical, dental and related services to community residents, with particular emphasis on serving the most in need.

Over the next three years the Center will expand and improve its health services. The Center will also expand its services to a broader segment of the community. More middle and upper income residents will use the Center's improved services. A new child development program will be operated in the Center's new building by either the Center or another agency. The total number of people served by the Center will increase from 4,800 this year to over 6,700 in year 3.

In year 1 the Center will move to a new facility developed to fit its needs, and will also provide services in several outreach locations.

The staff of the Center will be increased to provide those services, from 14.7 present full-time equivalents to 32.8 in year 3.

Center services will be financed through a broadened base of support. The Center will continue to request Federal, State and City grants, and will also request support from the County. Foundation grants will be used to fund the costs of moving into the new center and start-up costs of the child development program. Payments from patient fees, MA, insurance, Medicare and HMO payments will also increase with the Center's expanded target population and association with at least two major hospitals.

The Center's internal operations and Board of Directors will also be strengthened. The Center will have a strong management information system that has accounts receivable, accounts payable and statistical analysis capability.

In addition, the Center will strengthen its relationships with area hospitals, other community clinics and human service providers.

A. Service Description

Services	Description	Target Group Most in need	Other
1. Basic health care		70%	30%
a. Primary care	Internal medicine Family practice Pediatrics OB/gyn		
b. Other health services	Podiatry Ophthalmology Surgery Lab, x-ray		
c. Dental	Dental care		
d. Pharmacy	Prescriptions		
2. Related Services			
a. Health education	Screenings Classes: smoking, weight loss, exercise, etc. Health fairs, presentations	50%	50%
b. Transportation	Transportation to and from clinic	100%	0%
c. Child development/day care[2]	Day care with child development emphasis	45%	55%

B. Levels of Service

Services	Units of Service	Projected Service Levels			
		Base Year	Year 1	Year 2	Year 3
1. Basic Health Care					
a/b. Primary care and other health services	People served	4,300	4,485	5,085	5,890
	Visits	16,000	18,040	22,430	25,960
c. Dental	People served	500	550	800	800
	Visits	1,000	1,500	2,900	3,000
d. Pharmacy	Prescriptions	12,000	13,200	14,520	15,972
2. Related Services					
a. Health education (medical and dental)	People served	1,596	1,750	4,000	4,400
	Events	20	30	50	50
b. Transportation	Patient trips	3,840	4,800	6,000	6,500
c. Child development/ day care	Children served	0	0	40	40
	Capacity	0	0	30	30

-----

[1] See Appendix A for program assumptions
[2] A feasibility study will show whether the child development center should be operated by the Center or another organization.

STAFFING PLANS

Positions	Full-time equivalents			
	Base Year	Year 1	Year 2	Year 3
Basic health care:				
Medical Director	.8	.8	1.0	1.0
Internists	1.0	1.0	1.0	1.0
Family practice	-	1.0	1.0	1.0
Pediatrician	.1	.2	.5	1.0
OB/gyn[1]	-	1.0	1.0	1.0
Podiatrist	.2	.3	.5	.5
Ophthalmologic team[2] (in-kind)	(.1)	(.1)	(.1)	(.1)
Nurse practitioners[3]	1.0	1.0	1.5	2.0
Medical assistant	1.0	2.0	2.0	2.0
Nurse midwives (in-kind)[4]	(.1)	(.1)	(.1)	(.1)
Dentist	.5	.5	1.0	1.0
Dental hygienist	.3	.5	.75	1.0
Dental assistant	.7	.75	1.0	1.0
Dental team[5] (in-kind)	(.1)	(.1)	(.1)	(.1)
Pharmacist	1.0	1.0	1.0	1.0
Lab/x-ray technician	-	1.0	1.0	1.0
Total basic health staff	6.9	11.35	13.55	14.80
Related Services:				
Medical records technician	-	1.0	1.0	1.0
Health education coordinator (RN)	1.0	1.0	1.0	1.0
Pediatric nurse (day care)	-	-	2.0	2.0
Head teacher	-	-	1.0	1.0
Teacher's assistant	-	-	1.0	1.0
Teacher's aide	-	-	1.5	1.5
Cook	-	-	.4	.4
Van driver	1.0	1.0	1.0	1.0
Nutritionist	.1	.1	.1	.1
Total related services staff	2.1	3.1	9.0	9.0

Administration:	Full-time equivalents			
	Base Year	Year 1	Year 2	Year 3
Director	1.0	1.0	1.0	1.0
Financial manager	1.0	1.0	1.0	1.0
Grants manager	-	1.0	1.0	1.0
Office manager	1.0	1.0	1.0	1.0
Billing clerk	1.0	1.0	1.0	1.0
Receptionist	1.0	1.0	1.0	1.0
Patient information specialist	1.0	1.0	1.0	1.0
Office accountant	-	-	1.0	1.0
Clerical assistant	-	-	1.0	1.0
Total administrative staff	6.0	7.0	9.0	9.0
Total staff	15.00	21.45	31.55	32.80

-----

[1] Start date July, Year 1
[2] From County Medical Center
[3] Includes Clinic Coordinator
[4] From County Medical Center
[5] From the Army Reserve

FINANCIAL PLANS [1]

	Base Year	Year 1	Year 2	Year 3
A. Operating Budget				
Revenue:				
Federal grants (UHI)	$ 298,500	$ 305,000	$ 305,000	$ 305,000
State grants (Family planning, sexual assault, etc.)	17,307	93,061	98,061	25,000
City	78,532	78,532	78,532	78,532
County grant	-0-	62,024	62,024	62,024
Private foundation/corporation grants	10,542	30,000	40,000	30,000
United Way/Federated campaign	-0-	-0-	25,000	25,000
Health Education program income	-0-	500	2,000	5,000
Patient fees (Medical, Dental, Pharmacy)				
- sliding fee scale	35,947	97,360	148,232	226,764
- personal insurance	3,503	7,800	10,800	13,440
- Medical Assistance	101,246	108,160	140,250	152,640
- Medicare	4,849	10,920	15,750	22,400
- HMO's	5,000	7,852	12,060	24,320
- job voucher	3,000	5,600	-0-	-0-
Pharmacy	19,174	21,120	27,456	27,731
Contributions from Churches	-0-	30,000	10,000	-0-
Early Child Development project	-0-	-0-	96,980	104,000
Contributions for individuals	-0-	8,000	10,000	10,000
Miscellaneous income	3,990	8,100	9,000	9,500
Total Revenue	$ 581,590	$ 874,029	$1,091,145	$1,121,351

[1] See Appendix A for financial assumptions

Expenses:

	Base Year	Year 1	Year 2	Year 3
Personnel/fringe	$ 320,545	$ 374,986	$ 684,735	$ 790,972
Contractual services	157,125	234,850	52,000	10,000
Supplies/inventory	50,807	55,500	70,000	87,500
Space	38,000	59,000	96,000	96,000
Program support	14,000	30,000	50,000	50,000
Staff development	-0-	2,500	4,500	4,500
Equipment/maintenance	3,600	5,000	6,000	6,000
Equipment/purchase-lease	-0-	20,000	15,000	10,000
Total Expenses	$ 584,077	$ 781,836	$ 978,235	$1,054,972
Surplus/(Deficit)	$ (2,487)	$ 92,193	$ 112,910	$ 66,379

B. Building Budget

Item	Source	Base Year	Year 1	Year 2	Year 3
Assuming new site					
1. Moving and equipment costs (including furnishings)	Foundation grants Church grant	$ -0-	$ 15,000	$ -0-	$ 20,000
2. Leasehold improvements	City	-0-	48,000	-0-	-0-
3. Funds to purchase building (exercise purchase option)	Foundation grants Mortgage*	-0-	250,000	300,000	225,000
Total funds needed		$ -0-	$ 313,000	$ 300,000	$ 245,000

* Mortgage of up to $400,000 can be afforded if foundation goals are not reached.

FACILITY PLANS

In year 1 the Center will move into a four-story building at the corner of _____ and _____ . The space will be built to the Center's specifications by a private developer. The first floor of the facility will be clinic space, and the second floor will be offices. The ground floor will house a child development center operated by either the Center or another agency. The top floor will be leased by the developer to other organizations with complementary programs (e.g. mental health, services for women and children, financial counseling, etc.).

Each of the floors leased by the Center is 4,000 square feet; 12,000 square feet will be needed with the child development center or 8,000 square feet without it.

Most of the Center's services will be provided at the _____ location, but the Center will also provide outreach services at such locations as _____ Community Center, _____ Center, _____ and _____ .

The developer will finance the development and construction of the building. Leasehold improvements of clinic space will also be financed by the developer unless the Center wishes to raise money to cover those costs. The Center's rent will be no more than $8.00 per square foot (or $96,000 per year for 12,000 square feet) with a 3-5 year lease. If the Center chooses to raise money for leasehold improvements (approximately $48,000), the developer will reduce rent costs accordingly. The Center will also have an option to buy the facility. Money will be raised in years 1-3 to exercise that option in Year 4.

LINKAGES

Over the next three years the Center will strengthen its relationships with the following groups and organizations:

1. Outreach locations

    The Center will provide outreach medical, dental and health education services in several locations: _____ Community Center, _____ Center, _____ and _____ are likely locations.

2. County Medical Center

    The County Medical Center will continue to provide hospitalization and speciality care to our patients, as well as in-kind ophthalmologic and nurse midwife services.

3. _____ Hospital

    The Hospital will continue to provide hospitalization and speciality care to the Center's patients. Prepayment arrangements will be investigated.

4. Other hospitals/medical facilities

    Several other hospitals will also provide hospitalization to the Center's patients. Current providers also include _____ Hospital and _____ Hospital. A dental team from the Army Reserve will continue to provide in-kind services at the Center.

5. Other Community Health Clinics

    The Center will undertake several joint programs with other community health clinics, including joint community health education and research projects. In addition, the Center will provide pharmacy services to several clinics.

6. HMO's

   The Center will continue to serve as a provider clinic for the _____
   and _____ HMO. Reimbursement from at least one additional HMO will be arranged by year 2.

7. On-site services from other organizations

   _____ will continue to provide home health services to the Center's patients. _____
   will continue to provide counseling services. Several new services (women and children's program,
   financial counseling) will also be provided by other organizations in the new facility.

8. The Center will also increase its services to nonprofit (and for-profit) agencies in the provision of
   services to target populations and employees (e.g., physical examinations, health education, health
   screenings).

9. The Center will strengthen referral relationships with other service providers who can address the needs
   of our target population.

10. The Center will strengthen relationships with local affiliates of national health organizations.

IMPLEMENTATION PLANS

Steps	Responsible	By When

1. Determine the feasibility of operating a child development/day care center in the new facility.
  • Define questions and issues
  • Review findings
  • Outline course of action for the Center
	Planning Committee
	Executive Director
		October, This Year

2. Arrange new prepayment arrangements for health services.
  • Clarify unit costs and review pricing
  • Discuss options with several existing and new providers
  • Select providers
  • Negotiate contracts
	Associate Director	December, This Year

3. Clarify facilities plans.
  • Continue negotiations on preferred site
  • Proceed with plans for back-up site, if needed
	Executive Director	December, This Year

4. Continue to improve board functioning.
  • Review progress
  • Clarify responsibilities and composition desired for the future
	Executive Committee
	Nominations Committee
	Executive Director
		January, Year 1

5. Outline and implement development plans for the Center.
  • Complete program and overall financial plans
  • Outline a plan for raising needed monies
  • Implement plan
	Finance Committee
	Executive Director
	Assistant Director
		January, Year 1

6. Develop marketing plan.	Marketing/Community Relations Committee Executive Director	January, Year 1

Appendix C: Strategic Planning Worksheets

Benefits and Concerns

Instructions

1) List the benefits you expect from strategic planning as well as any concerns.
2) Note possible ways to overcome each of your concerns. Circle the best ideas.
3) Decide how you will proceed.

Benefits expected

Concerns

Ways to overcome concerns

DECIDE HOW YOU WILL PROCEED

☐ Full steam ahead ☐ With caution, addressing the concerns above ☐ Wait until a better time to begin ☐ Stop—don't proceed

Organize the Planning Effort

Instructions

Indicate how each of the following issues will be handled, then outline the steps, responsibilities, and timelines for developing your strategic plan.

1. You are developing a strategic plan for:
   □ Your total organization
   □ Only part of your organization (division, program)
   □ Total organization *and* each major program or division
   □ Other _____

2. For what period of time are you planning?
   □ Next 2 years
   □ Next 3 years
   □ Next 4 years
   □ Next 5 years
   □ Other (specify) _____

3. What critical issues do you hope the planning will address?

4. Time devoted to planning: which approach do you prefer?
   □ "What we can do in a limited time" approach: under 8 hours of planning meetings
   □ A compact approach: 10-20 hours of planning meetings
   □ A more extended approach: 24-40 hours of planning meetings
   □ Over 40 hours of planning meetings

5. Are you going to use a consultant or other resource persons in developing the plan?
   □ Yes
   □ No
   □ Unsure
   If so, what kind of help do you need? (Page 25 has suggestions.)

6. Will you use a planning team?
   □ Yes
   □ No
   □ Unsure
   If so, who will be on it? (check as many as apply)
   □ Board members
   □ Executive director/CEO
   □ Other staff
   □ Others: people in your field, clients or users, funders, etc.
   □ Consultant
   What size team might work best (5-8 people is common)? _____

7. Are there other people you want to involve?
   In the development of the plan?

   In the review of the plan?

Continued

8. Who within your organization will manage the overall planning effort?

9. Who will lead or chair the actual planning meetings?

10. By what date do you want to have the plan approved? _____

11. Outline the steps you will use in developing your plan. After outlining the process review it with the people involved, then make any changes needed.

Steps	Responsible	By when

History and Present Situation

Instructions

Review your organization's history and present situation. List any historical issues or trends that will need attention as you plan for the future.

Questions about Mission

Instructions

1) Describe below what you understand your organization's mission or purpose to be.
2) List any questions, ideas, or concerns you have about your present mission.
3) Consider what might be the best mission for your organization in the future. Describe what your organization might accomplish in coming years and who will be served.
4) Discuss your responses with the planning team and note areas of agreement and disagreement.

Present mission or purpose

Questions about current mission

Possible changes in mission for the future

What we want to accomplish

Who will be served—target group(s)

Opportunities and Threats

Instructions

1) List the major opportunities (O) and threats (T) that you believe your organization will face in the next 2-5 years that will determine whether it succeeds or fails.

2) Worksheets 5a and b may be useful if you wish to do a more detailed analysis of your customers or competition.

3) Combine your responses with those of other planning team members, then identify the 4-8 opportunities or threats that are most critical to your organization's future success.

Clients, customers, stakeholders

Competitors and allies

Social, cultural, economic, political, or technological forces

Clients, Customer, and Stakeholder Needs

Instructions

1) List the needs of present or potential "customers" that your organization might address. Note ideas for how your organization might meet those needs.
2) List the significant groups who have a stake in what you do (for example: funders, contractors, regulators, supporters). Note how you might meet their needs.
3) Transfer major opportunities and threats to the "clients, customers, stakeholders" column of Worksheet 5.

Clients, customers, users

Describe existing or possible new target groups	Their needs	Ways to meet those needs

Other stakeholders

List group or person	Their needs	Ways to meet those needs

Competitors and Allies

Instructions

1) List present and possible new competitors, what you compete for, then note your organization's relative advantages or disadvantages (price, image, quality, etc.).

2) List possible allies and how you might team up with each organization, person or group (e.g., joint program, merger, trade association).

3) Transfer major opportunities or threats to the "competitors and allies" column of Worksheet 5.

Competitors	Compete for	Your relative advantages	Your relative disadvantages
Existing			
New			

Allies	How might you team up?	

Strengths and Weaknesses

Instructions

1) List the major strengths and weaknesses of your organization as it faces the future.
2) Combine your responses with those of other planning team members. Note which strengths and weaknesses will be most critical to your organization's future success.

Strengths and assets

Weaknesses and liabilities

Critical Issues for the Future

Instructions

1) Review worksheets 4, 5 and 6; then list critical issues or choices that your organization faces over the next 2-5 years.

2) Combine your responses with those of other planning team members; then identify the 4-8 most critical issues.